W9-ATF-100

MORRILL ELEMENTARY SCHOOL

34880000824537

DATE DUE

977.4   Thompson, Kathleen.
Tho
     Michigan

PROPERTY OF
CHICAGO BOARD OF EDUCATION
DONALD L. MORRILL SCHOOL

STECK-VAUGHN
PORTRAIT OF AMERICA

Michigan

Copyright © 1996 Steck-Vaughn Company

c/l 1997

All rights reserved. No part of this book may be reproduced or utilized in any form or by any means, electronic or mechanical, including photocopying, recording, or by any information storage and retrieval system, without permission in writing from the copyright owner. Requests for permission to make copies of any part of the work should be mailed to: Copyright Permissions, Steck-Vaughn Company, P.O. Box 26015, Austin, Texas 78755.

15.95

Steck-Vaughn Company
  Executive Editor   Diane Sharpe
  Senior Editor   Martin S. Saiewitz
  Design Manager   Pamela Heaney
  Photo Editor   Margie Foster
  Electronic Cover Graphics Alan Klemp

Proof Positive/Farrowlyne Associates, Inc.
Program Editorial, Revision Development, Design, and Production

Consultant: Sandra Church, McNichols Library, Reference Department, University of Detroit-Mercy

Published by Raintree Steck-Vaughn Publishers, an imprint of Steck-Vaughn Company.

A Turner Educational Services, Inc. book. Based on the Portrait of America television series by R. E. (Ted) Turner.

Cover Photo: Detroit by © Uniphoto.

Library of Congress Cataloging-in-Publication Data

Thompson, Kathleen.
    Michigan / Kathleen Thompson.
       p.   cm. — (Portrait of America)
    "Based on the Portrait of America television series"—T.p. verso.
    "A Turner book."
    Includes index.
    ISBN 0-8114-7342-2 (library binding).—ISBN 0-8114-7447-X (softcover)
    1. Michigan—Juvenile literature. I. Title II. Series:
Thompson, Kathleen. Portrait of America.
F566.3.T48   1996
977.4—dc20   95-46310
                                                 CIP
                                                 AC

Printed and Bound in the United States of America

1 2 3 4 5 6 7 8 9 10 WZ 98 97 96 95

Acknowledgments
The publishers wish to thank the following for permission to reproduce photographs:
Pp. 7, 8 Michigan Travel Bureau, Lansing; p. 10 © Michael Reagan; p. 11 Mackinac Island State Park Commission; p. 12 Courtesy Pontiac Division, General Motors Corporation; p. 13 (both) William L. Clements Library/University of Michigan; p. 14 (top) Michigan Travel Bureau, Lansing, (bottom) Sophia Smith Collection; p. 15 (top) Courtesy Alfred Menza, (bottom) State Archives of Michigan; pp. 16, 17 Photos Courtesy Ford Motor Company; p. 18 (top) Chrysler Historical Collection, (bottom) UPI/Bettmann; p. 19 Gerald R. Ford Library; pp. 20, 21 © Earl Wolf/Michigan Department of Natural Resources; p. 22 (both) Michigan Travel Bureau, Lansing; p. 23 (left) Mackinac Island State Park Commission, (right) © Balthazar Korab/Grand Hotel; p. 24 © Superstock; p. 27 © Park Street; p. 28 (top) Michigan Farm Bureau, (bottom) Fayette State Park; p. 29 (top right, middle) Michigan Farm Bureau, (bottom) © S. Brooks-Miller/Fayette Historic Townsite; p. 30 First Independence National Bank; p. 31 Photo Courtesy William R. Eastabrook, courtesy of NARAS; p. 32 Lester Morgan's Cultural Gardens; p. 33 First Independence National Bank; p. 34 Tulip Time Festival; p. 36 (top) Cranbrook Academy of Art, (middle) Michigan Travel Bureau, Lansing; p. 37 Metropolitan Detroit Convention and Visitors Bureau; p. 38 (left) Metropolitan Detroit Convention and Visitors Bureau, (right) Motown Historical Museum; p. 39 (top) © Michael Reagan, (bottom) Michigan Travel Bureau, Lansing; pp. 40, 41 Interlochen Center For the Arts; p. 42 © Balthazar Korab, Ltd.; p. 44 Michigan Travel Bureau, Lansing; p. 46 One Mile Up; p. 47 (left) © Arthur C. Smith III/Grant Heilman Photography, (right) © Breck P. Kent/Earth Scenes, (bottom) One Mile Up.

STECK-VAUGHN
PORTRAIT OF AMERICA

Michigan

Kathleen Thompson

A Turner Book

RSVP

RAINTREE
STECK-VAUGHN
PUBLISHERS
The Steck-Vaughn Company

Austin, Texas

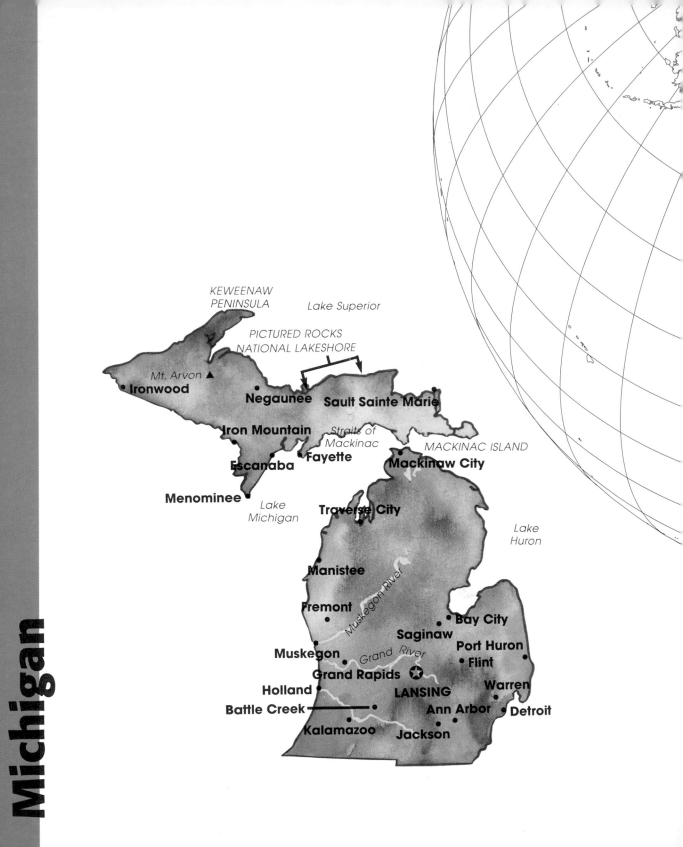

Michigan

KEWEENAW
PENINSULA

Lake Superior

PICTURED ROCKS
NATIONAL LAKESHORE

Mt. Arvon ▲

• Ironwood

• Negaunee

Sault Sainte Marie

Iron Mountain

Straits of
Mackinac

MACKINAC ISLAND

Escanaba

• Fayette

Mackinaw City

Menominee

Lake
Michigan

Traverse City

Lake
Huron

Manistee

Muskegon River

Fremont

Bay City

Saginaw

Port Huron

Muskegon

Grand River

Flint

Grand Rapids ✪

Holland

Warren

LANSING

Battle Creek

Ann Arbor

Detroit

Kalamazoo

Jackson

Contents

Introduction

Thousands of years ago, glaciers crept down from the north and left an imprint on America. One result is Michigan—also known as the water wonderland. Four of the five Great Lakes border on Michigan. Over 11,000 natural inland lakes and hundreds of rivers and streams decorate the state's interior. All that water has helped the people of Michigan with their industry, too. The rivers are useful for hydroelectric power and transportation. Ships carry Michigan products to Wisconsin, Ohio, Illinois, New York, Indiana, Minnesota, and Canada. All these places can be reached from Michigan through the Great Lakes. Best of all, wherever you are in Michigan, you don't have to travel very far to throw out your baited hook or dip your toes in Michigan's most abundant natural resource—water.

With so much water available to them, Michigan residents have gained an appreciation for water sports, such as sailboat racing.

Michigan

ERECTED TO PERPETUATE THE MEMORY OF THE
PIONEER LUMBERMEN OF MICHIGAN THROUGH
WHOSE LABORS WAS MADE POSSIBLE THE
DEVELOPMENT OF THE PRAIRIE STATES

The Great Lakes State

About 15,000 years ago, the Michigan region was covered by glaciers, which carved out the Great Lakes. The distinctive shape of the state today is due to their great forces. When the ice retreated, an ancient people moved into the region. They lived in the Upper Peninsula and what is now Isle Royale, in the northern section of Lake Superior. There they discovered copper, which they turned into tools and household items. These ancient people may have been the first people in the Western Hemisphere to work with metal. Later, around A.D. 200, another group called the Hopewells lived in the Michigan region. These Native Americans left behind burial mounds, which are found all over the state. After a few hundred years, the Hopewell civilization left. No one knows why.

By the time the first Europeans came to the region, Michigan was home to about 15,000 people. The Menominee and the Chippewa lived in the Upper Peninsula. Ottawa, Potawatomi, Miami, and Huron

More than ten thousand lumberjacks worked in Michigan forests during the mid-1800s. The Lumbermen's Monument, near Oscoda, recalls their service to the state.

Mackinac Bridge crosses the Straits of Mackinac, connecting the Upper and Lower peninsulas of Michigan.

lived in the Lower Peninsula. Most of these Native Americans hunted elk, deer, and other animals of the forest. They fished the region's inland lakes and rivers and traveled the Great Lakes in canoes designed to carry as many as twenty people.

Then, in about 1620, a French explorer named Étienne Brulé began exploring the Great Lakes. He moved up Lake Huron to the waterfalls and rapids that connected Lake Huron and Lake Superior, along the border between what are now the United States and Canada.

More than ten years later, another French explorer, Jean Nicolet, explored the Michigan region. He passed through the channel that connects Lake Huron and Lake Michigan, between the Upper and Lower peninsulas of what is now the state of Michigan. Today this channel is called the Straits of Mackinac, pronounced *Mackinaw*.

The French traded furs with the Native Americans and tried to convert them to Catholicism. Father Jacques Marquette created the first permanent French settlement at Sault Sainte Marie in 1668. In 1701 the French established a fort in the area that is now Detroit. The fort was a center for the fur trade. Around 1715 the French built a fort at the Straits of Mackinac, called Fort Michilimackinac. It too was a center for the fur trade.

In 1754 a war began between France and Great Britain. Because Native Americans took sides with either the French or the British in this war, the war became known as the French and Indian War. Native Americans in Michigan fought on the side of the French. When the British won the war in 1763, the French had to give up all the land east of the Mississippi River. Michigan was now controlled by the British.

Michigan's Native Americans didn't accept the British. Pontiac, an Ottawa chief, tried to force the British out. In early 1763, Native Americans captured Fort Michilimackinac and other important British posts and laid siege to Detroit for almost six months. But in the end, the British soldiers won.

The British also had problems with their colonists along the East Coast. In 1776 the colonists went to war against Great Britain in the Revolutionary War.

The French built Fort Michilimackinac in 1715, at the site of present-day Mackinac City.

Chief Pontiac led the fight against British rule.

Detroit was a British stronghold, and it provided soldiers, ammunition, and even raiding parties to help the British forces. The colonists won the war in 1783. In the treaty that ended the war, Michigan officially became a part of the new United States of America. Nonetheless, it took a second treaty, in 1794, to remove the British from Michigan.

In 1805 Congress established the Michigan Territory, which included all of the present-day Lower Peninsula and about half of the Upper Peninsula. Native Americans continued to fight a losing battle to keep their land. In 1807 under great pressure from the settlers and the government, the Huron signed treaties giving their land in southeast Michigan to the Americans.

Then the War of 1812 broke out between the Americans and the British. The British forced Detroit and Fort Michilimackinac to surrender. But the Americans started to win battles. The war ended in 1814, and the British retreated into Canada. Michigan was now under complete control of the United States.

After the War of 1812, more settlers moved into Michigan. In 1818 the United States government sold public lands in Michigan to settlers for about four dollars an acre. Between 1819 and 1821, Native Americans gave up more land in southern and central Michigan. Steamship travel on Lake Erie made it easier for families to settle in the territory. Michigan built roads, canals, and railroads so people could travel inland.

In 1820 roads were built between Detroit and two inland cities, Pontiac and Mount Clemens. Shipping expanded on the Great Lakes. The Erie Canal opened in 1825, completing a direct water route from New York to Lake Erie. Now European immigrants landing in New York and New Englanders looking for fertile land could travel to the Great Lakes by way of the canal. Roads connected Detroit to Chicago and to two other Michigan cities, Saginaw and Port Huron. Michigan settlements followed these roads.

In 1835 Michigan applied to Congress for statehood. But there were disagreements with Ohio and Wisconsin about state boundaries. Michigan claimed a piece of land called the Toledo Strip. Ohio wanted that strip because it would give them access to Lake Michigan. The solution was a compromise. Ohio got the Toledo Strip, and Congress took from Wisconsin a section of today's Upper Peninsula and gave it to Michigan. In 1837 Michigan became the twenty-sixth state to join the Union.

Also during this time, Michiganians were involved in the "Underground Railroad." This wasn't a real railroad. It was a system for helping runaway slaves escape by traveling north, sometimes all the way to Canada. People hid runaways in churches and private homes and gave them clothes, money, or food to help them on their way. Since Detroit was separated from Canada only by a river, the city was an important destination

above. Detroit is in Wayne County, which is named for General Anthony Wayne, a leader in the Revolutionary War.

below. This diagram portrays Fort Lernoult in Detroit, which the British used to control the region until 1796.

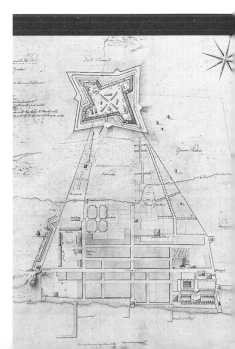

These are the Tahquamenon Falls in the Upper Peninsula.

Sojourner Truth bore four children as a slave—all were taken from her and sold. After she escaped, she made her home in Battle Creek. She traveled all over the country, talking about her life as a slave.

for the Underground Railroad. One escaped slave named Sojourner Truth lived in Battle Creek. She traveled all over the country, describing her life as a slave to raise funds to help other slaves leave the country.

After gaining statehood, economic prosperity continued in Michigan. Logging and mining were important industries. In early 1842, Native American treaties gave up Isle Royale and Keweenaw Peninsula, on Lake Superior. Only two years later, an "iron rush" began in the Upper Peninsula, near Negaunee. Then the settlers discovered copper in the Keweenaw Peninsula, just as the Native Americans had centuries earlier. Large ships moved the metals across the Great Lakes. But the falls at Sault Sainte Marie were a barrier to shipping. So in 1855 the "Soo locks" were finished. The locks made it possible for ships to get to markets in places such as Detroit and Chicago.

When the Civil War broke out in 1861, Michigan sent nearly one hundred thousand soldiers to fight for the Union, including the First Michigan Colored Infantry. African Americans from other states and even from Ontario, Canada, were members of this group.

The logging business became even more important to Michigan after the Civil War. There was a great demand for lumber, especially in the prairie states where trees were scarce. As settlers moved west, lumber from Michigan enabled them to build homes

By 1849 there were more than 550 sawmills operating in Michigan. Timber was falling at a rate of 33,000 acres a year.

and towns. By 1870 the state was producing more lumber than any other state. By 1882 there were 32 railroads into the logging areas of the state. Michigan was booming. In 1830 it had about thirty thousand citizens. By 1870 there were nearly two million!

Soon, factories in the state were making paper, furniture, breakfast cereal, buggies, bicycles, and railroad cars. Even so, agriculture remained the state's largest source of income. Prosperity attracted more people. During the last 25 years of the nineteenth century, Michigan's population doubled. This was a time of many reforms. Governor Hazen S. Pingree was elected in 1897. Under his leadership, the legislature passed many progressive laws, including compensation for workers injured on the job.

Between 1820 and 1850, thousands of families immigrated to Michigan. Most were from Germany.

By the end of the 1800s, the logging industry was dying out, simply because almost all of Michigan's forests had been cut down. A new industry was ready to take its place, however. In 1886 R. E. Olds drove his first steam-powered automobile down the streets of Lansing. By 1896 Olds had switched to a gasoline-powered engine and founded the Olds Motor Works in Detroit. In 1903 Henry Ford opened the Ford Motor Company to produce his automobiles. All over the state, in cities like Flint and Lansing, buggy and bicycle factories became automobile factories. Michigan became the center of a huge new industry.

In 1917 the United States joined the Allies to fight in World War I against Germany. That war increased Michigan's prosperity. The automobile factories produced armored vehicles, trucks, and other military products. People moved from the farms and also migrated from the South to work in these factories.

The Great Depression swept across the nation in the 1930s. People lost their savings and their jobs. The automobile factories were forced to lay off more and more workers. By 1933 about half of all auto industry workers were out of work. In 1932 Franklin D. Roosevelt was elected President of the United States. He proposed to get people back to work through "the New Deal." In Michigan this meant that the federal government set up more than a hundred Civilian Conservation Corps (CCC) camps. The CCC hired young men to do things like plant trees and fight fires. The Works Progress Administration (WPA) hired half a million people for public works projects in Michigan.

Henry Ford poses with the "quadricycle," which was his very first car.

All over the state, as in other states, there are parks and buildings constructed by the WPA.

In 1935 workers who were tired of bad working conditions and unfair treatment by factory owners organized a labor union called the United Automobile Workers (UAW). In 1936 the UAW went on strike at factories owned by Chevrolet and Fisher Body in Flint. The workers in the UAW wanted collective bargaining. In other words, they wanted to bargain as a unified group rather than as individuals.

Ford revolutionized manufacturing with his creation of the moving assembly line. This 1913 photo shows the line at Ford's Highland Park assembly plant.

In Flint the owners of the General Motors plant turned down workers' demands, so the workers locked themselves inside the factories and refused to come out. The National Guard was sent to remove them, but the workers fought back. They believed that they were fighting for more than just higher pay. They were fighting for the right to have some say in their own lives. Finally, in February 1937, the workers won the right to collective bargaining with the company. Between 1937 and 1941, the UAW sponsored strikes with other companies until all automobile company owners agreed to negotiate with their workers in this way. This was very important for labor unions across the nation, because they could also get collective bargaining.

The United States joined World War II in 1941, and Michigan's economy soon received a boost. The

During World War II, auto manufacturing plants switched over to producing materials for the war effort.

Coleman Young was elected to five terms of office as mayor of Detroit.

military needed jeeps, trucks, tanks, and airplanes, and Detroit factories could make them. The federal government bought more military vehicles from Michigan than from any other state.

The auto industry went through a boom period after the war. One reason was that returning veterans were eager to buy new products such as automobiles. Another reason was that many families wanted to move to the suburbs. The automobile made it possible for people to commute to jobs in the cities. The boom in the car industry encouraged African Americans to migrate from the South to work in Michigan's automobile plants. The economy was so dependent on the automobile business that when slow economic times came in the late 1950s, unemployment was a severe problem. This pattern has repeated itself several times since then.

Beginning in the 1950s, more and more people across the country moved from cities to suburbs. Social problems occurred because wealthier people moved to the suburbs and poorer people remained in the cities.

For instance, the cities did not have enough money to pay for schools and other social programs. In 1963 George Romney was elected governor. He addressed some of Michigan's social problems. To provide money for improving education and public welfare programs, he led the state legislature to set up an income tax law.

But these changes didn't solve the problems of poverty, poor housing, and racism in Detroit and other Michigan cities. In 1967 these problems led to riots in Detroit. Forty-three people died, and hundreds were injured. Property worth millions of dollars was destroyed. After the riots the state passed an open-housing law. This law said that when people rented or sold a house, they could not discriminate against anyone because of race, religion, or nationality. Nonetheless, racial problems still continued to plague Michigan cities.

In the late 1970s and the 1980s, the automobile business changed a great deal. Cars made in Japan outsold cars made by American companies. This change hit Michigan's economy hard because of its dependence on the automobile industry. But American companies learned some lessons, and they are making a comeback. In addition, Michigan has begun developing businesses that aren't tied to the automobile industry.

Michigan faces great challenges with its cities, the economy, and the environment. But Michiganians have seen the good life when the automobile industry was flourishing. They look forward to new businesses, a renewed auto industry, and a new century in which to grow.

Michigan's Gerald Ford was the first President to serve without having been elected as either President or Vice President. Ford was named Vice President by President Richard Nixon when Spiro Agnew resigned, and then became President when Nixon also resigned.

19

Legends of the Land

Years ago the area now known as Michigan was mainly inhabited by Native Americans. They hunted and fished in the area's woods and waters. As in any other culture, the Native Americans made up names for their surroundings. Sometimes these names came from legends. The Sleeping Bear Dune on the shore of Lake Michigan got its name this way.

According to Chippewa legend, a mother bear and two cubs were trying to escape a forest fire in Wisconsin. When they reached the shore of Lake Michigan, they began to swim. They swam across the lake to Michigan. The mother bear swam far out beyond her cubs, who she thought were right behind. She reached the far side of the lake and climbed up on a bluff to watch for her cubs. The cubs never came into sight. In great sadness, the mother bear waited there until she died. The legend claims the Great Spirit put a sand mound where she died, a mound called Sleeping Bear Dune.

The Great Lakes region is famous for its changeable weather. An Ottawa legend explains why the weather in Michigan is the way it is. Once two brothers named Na-na-bo-jo and Pee-puck-e-wis decided to have a running contest. These brothers had special powers, but it was Na-na-bo-jo who first took the lead. As he ran the sun shone, flowers bloomed, and animals played. All summer Na-na-bo-jo stayed in the lead. Pee-puck-e-wis, who trailed behind, was beginning to get angry. He was a mischievous character and decided to put a stop to the pleasant weather his brother enjoyed.

The sand bluffs of Sleeping Bear Dune rise 465 feet above Lake Michigan.

The Porcupine Mountains got their name from Michigan's Native Americans. They thought the mountains' rough ridges looked like crouching porcupines.

He asked the south wind to howl through the land and make the trees lose their leaves. Then he asked the east wind to bring rain, hail, and frost. He called upon dark clouds to blot out the sun and make it difficult for his brother to find his way. By this time it was October, and Na-na-bo-jo had reached the shores of Lake Michigan. He rested there, and the weather turned warm and peaceful. The trees on the shore were different colors of red, gold, and orange. Pee-puck-e-wis soon found his brother, however, and forced him to move on by sending for the north wind, which brought snow, wind, and ice. Whenever Na-na-bo-jo smiled, however, the sun would shine and the winds would calm down. The legend explains why the sun can shine in the depth of winter or there can be a thunderstorm in the heart of summer—it is because the brothers are still running their race.

These legends are a reminder of how much Native American culture was based on the natural environment. Native Americans did not feel that a dune or the weather were separate from humans. To Native Americans, everything and everyone was a part of nature.

Living in the Straits

In the waters of the Straits of Mackinac (pronounced "Mak-i-naw") is an island that has played a role in almost all of Michigan's history. Native Americans, French, and British lived on this island before it became a part of the United States.

Native Americans called the island *Michilimackinac*, which means "Great Turtle." Today it is called Mackinac Island. Jean Nicolet, a French explorer, passed through the Straits of Mackinac in about 1630. A monument to him stands at Arch Rock on the island. The Early Missionary Bark Chapel is a copy of the chapels of early French Catholic missionaries.

The British built Fort Mackinac on the island to protect the straits from the colonists during the Revolutionary War. In 1817 the United States finally took control of the fort and most of the surrounding region from the British. The United States continued to use the fort until 1894. Today the fort is a state park, restored to its original condition. Park workers wear wigs and uniforms and carry muskets to reenact

Arch Rock is a natural formation. Near it stands the monument to Jean Nicolet, a French explorer.

When you tour Mackinac Island, you don't rent a car, you rent a carriage!

These costumed tour guides work at Old Fort Mackinac. The cannons at the fort are shot off every half hour during the summer.

A horse-drawn cab stops at the Grand Hotel.

life at the fort in the eighteenth and nineteenth centuries.

In the early 1800s, the American Fur Company gained control of the fur trade in the Great Lakes and had its headquarters on Mackinac Island. This company was founded by John Jacob Astor. The Astors became one of the richest families in the United States. The headquarters and some of the original papers of the fur company are preserved at the Stuart House Museum on the island.

In the nineteenth century, wealthy families began to visit the island for summer vacations. To serve them, the Grand Hotel was built on a hill high above the rest of the town. Today this beautiful old hotel is still open, surrounded by gardens and lush lawns. Visitors are impressed by its famous front porch, one of the longest front porches in the world.

To visit Mackinac Island today, you must fly or go there by boat. You can't take a car because cars aren't allowed on the island except for emergency services. Instead, people travel by horse-and-buggy or by larger horse-drawn carriages. Bicycles are also allowed—because they don't have engines! Mackinac Island is a resort spot, so it has shops and tourist sights. But it's good to remember that this island has always been honored because of its position on the strait—and because of its beauty.

Economy on Wheels

For most of this century, the automobile industry drove Michigan's economy. But during the last twenty years the industry—and Michigan—have suffered a decline. Today service industries bring the most money into the state—about 65 percent of the state's gross state product.

In service industries, workers don't produce things you can see and touch. Instead, they perform services for other people. Maybe they work in a bank, a real estate office, or an insurance office. Accountants and tax advisors also work in service industries. In Michigan, banking, finance, and real estate make up the largest part of the service economy.

The second most important service group in Michigan is made up of personal services. Doctors, dentists, and nurses are part of this group. So are people who repair cars, clean carpets, and run community recreation centers. Some personal services are very specialized, such as advertising agencies.

This is a production line for automobile engines in Lansing. No state produces more cars and trucks than Michigan.

Next comes retail trade, which is selling things to customers, and wholesale trade, supplying the goods to sell to customers. Wholesale companies sell things like automobile parts to dealers and repair shops. Retail companies include car dealerships, department stores, grocery stores, and restaurants.

The last service group is people who work for the federal, state, and local governments. They may give driver's license tests, or work as librarians, police officers, or dog catchers.

Manufacturing is the next biggest contributor to Michigan's economy. It brings in about 28 percent of Michigan's income. The most important manufacturing activity is still motor vehicles—all kinds of automobiles, buses, and trucks. People don't just manufacture the completed car, however. They also manufacture parts such as fenders, rearview mirrors, brakes, and turn signals. They also manufacture the machines that make cars. Many of the cities in southern Michigan wouldn't exist if it weren't for automobiles and all the things it takes to make them.

The second and third largest areas of manufacturing are nonelectric machinery, such as office machines and equipment for working metals, and fabricated metal products, such as hammers, screwdrivers, and pots and pans.

Chemicals are a large part of the state's manufacturing economy, too. The chemical industry may have gotten its start with the founder of Dow Chemical Company in Midland. When he was just a beginning chemist, Herbert Henry Dow became famous for accidentally blowing up at least three chemical plants before 1897. That's when he founded today's company. Today Dow is world famous. Other chemical companies, such as the Upjohn Company, make medicines and drugs.

Michigan is an important food-processing state, too. Food processors take agricultural products like corn and turn them into other food products. Your breakfast cornflakes were probably made in Battle Creek. That's where both Kellogg and Post cereals are made. Another important food processor makes only baby food. In 1927 Dan Gerber of Fremont was the first person to make commercially prepared baby food. Today his company sells Gerber baby food all over the world.

Food processors need agricultural products to process. Some of those come from Michigan's 63,000 farms. The southwestern part of Michigan is one of the

In 1894, in Battle Creek, health food enthusiast W. K. Kellogg created his corn flakes by accident. Today Battle Creek is called the "Cereal Bowl of America."

Wheat is grown in the central section of the Lower Peninsula.

When Fayette was booming, it was a place where iron ore was smelted into "pig iron," bars of iron that were easy to ship.

best places on the continent to grow fruit. In the summer, orchards are thick with peaches, cherries, and plums. In the fall there are apples. The state's fields also produce cantaloupes, strawberries, and blueberries, and its vineyards produce grapes for eating and for making wine.

Most of Michigan's minerals are found in the Upper Peninsula. By the 1800s almost all of the state's high-grade iron ore was gone. Today these mines produce a lower grade of iron called taconite, but the state is still the source of one third of all the iron produced in the United States. Michigan's Lower Peninsula provides petroleum and natural gas, the state's most important minerals. Michigan is also a big producer of Portland cement, a major ingredient in concrete. Altogether mining brings in about as much income as agriculture.

Michigan is a beautiful state, and tourism now brings in more than $16 million a year. Some people come to hunt or fish. Others simply come to enjoy the natural beauty of Michigan's lakes and forests.

Michigan's economy is more diversified now than it has been for about a hundred years. The automobile industry is on the rebound, too. These things make it clear that Michigan is ready to tackle the challenges of the twenty-first century.

Fresh, canned, and dried tart cherries are a prime Michigan fruit.

Most grapes grown in Michigan vineyards are used to produce wine. Michigan ranks fifth in the country in wine production.

The former iron-ore town of Fayette is preserved as a state park.

A Way Out and Up

No one has ever said that Detroit was an easy city in which to grow up. Just ask Don Davis. He grew up in one of Detroit's toughest neighborhoods, and he knew it would be hard to succeed there or anywhere else in the city. He knew he needed to find a way out. When he discovered music, he knew he'd found it. He remembered those days well. "I was able to get my hands on the saxophone and learn how to play it. Was able to borrow my cousin's trumpet. Learned how to play it. So finally, after I ran out of instruments to play, I decided that I really wanted to play a guitar."

No one has ever said that music was an easy way to make a living. Don Davis knew about that, too. It took a long time before he was a professional musician. He began to play in clubs around Detroit. He also wrote songs. Then came the time when he had the chance to have his music recorded in a real recording studio. When the technicians played back the music, Davis was astounded. "They played the guitar music back through these enormous speakers . . . and it was ten times bigger than what I was hearing before it got on tape. I mean, I fell in love with it. . . . I mean, how could something come back so big?"

Don Davis is the major shareholder in First Independence Bank.

Marilyn McCoo and Billy Davis, Jr., received a Grammy Award for their Don Davis-produced hit single, "You Don't Have to Be a Star."

Davis decided that he wanted to make that happen for other Detroit musicians, not just for himself. That recording studio was more than just a place to play music. It was what Don Davis wanted. He told the studio owner that. He said that someday he was going to buy that studio. And that's just what he did, although it took a while.

Davis needed to borrow money to buy the studio, and more than one bank thought that the music business was just too risky. They wouldn't approve his loans. But Don Davis didn't give up. Ultimately, he became the owner of United Sound Systems, Inc.

So Davis began producing records. He had a goal in mind for his music business. He wanted to produce music by African American artists that would appeal to all audiences, not just African Americans. And he did it. He's especially proud of one of the records he produced because it won a Grammy and sold a million records. Davis went on to make United Sound one of the ten top independent record producers.

But that wasn't quite enough. Davis needed a new challenge. He looked around for a business that could help him widen his own perspective and could also help his community. One way to do that was through a bank. He remembered how hard it had been to borrow money to get his music production business started. So, Davis

31

The housing units at Lester Morgan's Cultural Gardens were built within Detroit's Cultural Center.

bought a majority interest in Detroit's First Independence National Bank.

First Independence was a special bank to Don Davis. For one thing it had been the first bank to turn down his request for a loan all those years ago. More importantly, all of the shareholders of First Independence were members of Detroit's African American community, and they understood many of Davis's goals. He could carry out his plans to help other small-business

people get started, just as his early loans had helped him. He could also work with private construction companies to restore and rebuild housing in Detroit's inner city.

Davis worked with city officials, African American churches, and other organizations to make the dream come true. In 1992 Lester Morgan's Cultural Gardens opened to new residents. This complex of more than 130 townhouses and apartments was unique because it was built in Detroit's central area, where no new housing had been built for a number of years. Forty of the units were for low-income residents. The project met the needs of the city and the needs of the people who moved in.

But then the economy in Detroit slowed down. When the economy of a city is very slow, it isn't easy to make money, even in the banking business. It's especially hard in Detroit because the city is so dependent on the automobile industry. When things go bad in that industry, things go bad everywhere else. So the bank went through some difficult times. But Davis isn't someone who gives up easily. Somewhere along the line, maybe in that tough neighborhood where he grew up, Don Davis learned the secret to success in business. "I would say the most important thing about an entrepreneur is the ability not to quit. And no matter how many times you get knocked down, to get up and keep fighting. And at the end of the fight, the referee will tell you that you lost. Then the entrepreneur will change the rules. And keep going."

First Independence National Bank became a center for financing small Detroit businesses run by women and minorities.

Michigan Culture— A Way of Life

Detroit has always been the center of Michigan culture because Detroit has always been the state's biggest city. In the early days, traveling theater companies gave performances in Detroit. The city built an opera theater before the Civil War. It built its symphony hall in 1919, and world-famous musicians still perform there. Detroit is the home of the Henry Ford Museum. It has exhibits of every kind to explore the history of industry in America, from a kitchen sink to airplane propellers to an 1890s shoe shop. The museum also features many hands-on, interactive exhibits.

Detroit is also home to a very special school. In 1920 George Boothe founded the Cranbrook Academy of Art in order to encourage freedom of expression in art and design. At Cranbrook you'll also find a planetarium and the Institute of Science. For a number of years, the Academy of Art was headed by Eliel Saarinen and his son Eero. Both Saarinens were Greek immigrants, but more importantly, both are still recognized as two of the world's greatest architects,

Immigrants from the Netherlands settled Holland, Michigan, in 1847. Today thousands of visitors come to see tulips blossom every May during the Holland Tulip Time Festival.

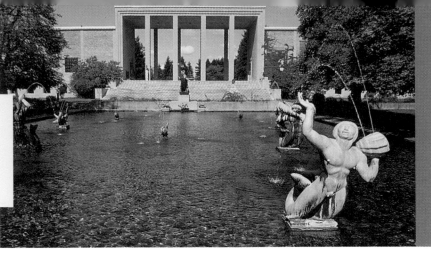

The Cranbrook Academy of Art in Bloomfield Hills was designed by architect Eliel Saarinen to combine art, architecture, and nature.

Henry Ford bought entire buildings if he thought they were historically important. Thomas Edison's laboratory, where Edison invented the electric lightbulb, is now located at Greenfield Village.

especially Eero. One of the buildings that Eliel Saarinen is famous for is the Tabernacle Church of Christ in Columbus, Indiana. His son is known for structures such as the St. Louis Arch in Missouri.

Detroit isn't the only place in Michigan where there are operas, museums, and academies of art, however. Symphony orchestras in Grand Rapids and Muskegon have national reputations. Lansing is the home of the Michigan Historical Museum, which uses huge murals and artifacts to explain the state's history. There is a re-creation of an old copper mine that is large enough to walk through. You can learn about shipping and sailing on the Great Lakes at Sault Sainte Marie's Valley Camp Museum. Among the exhibits there, you can see one of the only things that rescuers ever found when they searched for the sunken oreboat *Edmund Fitzgerald*—a lifeboat that was torn in two when the ship went down. In Kalamazoo's Aviation History

Museum you can see old World War II fighter planes and take a ride in the museum's flight simulator.

But early settlers who worked the land, dug the ore, and sailed the Great Lakes had other ways to celebrate their culture. The very first state fair ever held in the United States was held in Michigan. A fair is an event where people display the skills they use in their daily lives. They show the animals they tend, the food they prepare, and the quilts and other home products they make. They also display the machines they use to grow their crops and till their fields. A fair usually reflects the home life of people.

Ferryboats are still used to reach the Manitou Islands, Beaver Island, Mackinac Island, and Isle Royale.

Festivals are held in Michigan that reflect different cultures. Holland, Michigan, in the southwestern corner of the state, holds a Tulip Festival every spring. This festival is famous for celebrating the Dutch ancestry of Holland's people. Acres of tulips are in bloom. Dancers wear traditional Dutch costumes with wooden shoes as they perform traditional dances. On Beaver Island in Lake Michigan's northern waters, people cherish homes and traditions passed down by Irish immigrants. There's a Finnish festival in Calumet, a Bavarian festival in Frankenmuth, and a Celebration of African American Emancipation at Greenfield Village in Dearborn, near Detroit.

Some kinds of cultural activities are thought of as "everyday culture," or mass culture, because they

above. Big things start small. This was the original Hitsville USA office in the 1960s. The Motown Historical Museum now occupies the house.

right. The Supremes are the singers most associated with the Motown Sound.

appeal to so many people. Michigan is home to a very special part of mass culture—the music known all over the world as the Motown Sound. All during the 1960s, Motown's tiny Hitsville USA recording studio turned out hit records with a slick urban rhythm. Its founder, Berry Gordy, wanted a studio that would not only feature Detroit's African American musicians and singers but that would also pay them a fair wage for their work. And that's what he did. There's a long list of performers who got their start at Motown—people like Stevie Wonder, Marvin Gaye, the Temptations, and the Supremes. Detroit is still a center for rock 'n' roll and rhythm and blues.

Michigan's landscape is probably the most important contributor to the state's culture. Michigan has more freshwater coastline than any other state. There are more than eleven thousand inland lakes and 36,350 miles of rivers. In the Upper Peninsula, there are over 150 waterfalls. You can stand anywhere in Michigan and not be more than six miles away from water. That makes Michigan a place where people spend a lot of time outdoors throughout the year. For instance, there are more golf courses in Michigan than any other state in the country. People can camp in the state and national forests, ski, toboggan, and snowmobile in the hills, or they can sail and canoe in the waters. In Michigan people fish, whether it's for trout, sunfish, and bluegills in the inland lakes, or perch and coho salmon in the Great Lakes.

So Michigan is a state that values all kinds of culture. It is a place to learn and a place to play, a place to celebrate the past as well as the present, and a place to look to the future.

Michigan's Great Lakes shoreline is 3,288 miles long.

Cross-country skiing is only one of Michigan's popular winter sports.

Filling the Woods with Music

In the 1920s Dr. Joseph Maddy was teaching at the University of Michigan, in Ann Arbor, west of Detroit. Maddy was convinced that boys and girls in high school could become fine musicians. All they needed was the time and the attention of great teachers. So in 1927 he and a friend, Thomas Giddings, founded the National High School Orchestra Camp. They set up the orchestra camp at what had been a hunting lodge just south of Traverse City, on the northern Lake Michigan side of the Lower Peninsula. Their music camp has become far more successful that they probably ever dreamed.

Today the camp is known as the Interlochen Arts Camp. Every summer more than 1,400 middle school and high school students come from all over the world to spend up to eight weeks at Interlochen. All they need is talent. Although the camp is expensive, there are generous scholarship programs. Students take classes in music, visual arts, drama, creative writing, or dance. Their teachers are highly accomplished professionals in their fields.

The camp has grown in many ways in order to best serve its students. The campus of the camp covers 1,200 acres of land. There are

The Interlochen Arts Camp is the largest, best-known, and most successful camp of its kind in the United States.

Music students at Interlochen practice one to four hours every day.

Both the school and the summer camp offer some of the very best arts programs in the country. And how successful is Interlochen? More than fifty thousand people have gone to Interlochen since it began in 1928. Its music students play in symphony orchestras all over the world. Its drama graduates include Hollywood actors such as Tom Hulce, Meredith Baxter, and Linda Hunt. Its singers include major opera star Jessye Norman. Although the writers camp began only about ten years ago, its students have already won over 250 national awards. Not a bad record for a school that started off as a hunting lodge in the north woods.

two outdoor concert halls, a theater, an art gallery, an indoor auditorium, a chapel and recital hall, and a complex of buildings that contain classrooms and studios.

In 1962 Dr. Maddy achieved another dream. He opened the Interlochen Arts Academy, a year-round boarding school for young art students. At a boarding school, students live at the school during the entire school year, not just during the summer camp.

A guest artist teaches a class at Interlochen.

Looking Forward

Michigan faces its future with an abundance of resources and also a number of challenges. One of its biggest challenges is how it can become less dependent on the automobile industry. That change is happening with new companies in computers and high-tech robotics. This time Michiganians are determined to build an economy based on many different industries. It's clear that they have the skilled workers to make their goal a reality.

There is a second challenge: to make sure that all of Michigan's citizens, including the poor, share in the state's economy. In the past that has been a problem in cities all over the country, not just in Michigan. Michiganians have seen their cities suffer riots of protest in the past. They're working hard to try to change the conditions that prompted people to react that way. You can see their hopes for the future in the Renaissance Center in Detroit. Renaissance means rebirth. Everyone is working toward this goal.

Detroit built its Renaissance Center to improve the downtown area. The Renaissance Center is one of the largest urban renewal projects in the history of the United States.

Pictured Rocks are colorful limestone cliffs along the Lake Superior coastline. The mysterious shapes have been carved out by wind and water.

Michigan has to face the challenge of maintaining its environment. People in Michigan have already done a great deal. Michiganians have now reforested more than half the state. But there are other problems left. They have to find ways to clean up the toxic waste left behind by paper mills and mining. They have to keep on improving the quality of their water. And they have to preserve the environment that draws so many visitors to the state, year after year. It's hard to balance things. How do you keep an environment beautiful when more people and more cars come to visit every year?

People in Michigan are determined to find the balance. They value the new cars that come off Detroit's production lines. But they also value the moose and the wolves on Isle Royale, far north in Lake Superior.

100 B.C. The Hopewell enter what is now southwestern Michigan.

A.D. 1620 Étienne Brulé is the first European to enter Michigan.

1634 Jean Nicolet passes through the Straits of Mackinac.

1668 The first permanent French settlement is founded by Father Jacques Marquette at Sault Sainte Marie.

1701 Antoine de la Mothe Cadillac founds Fort Pontchartrain at what is now Detroit.

1763 Ottawa chief Pontiac leads a rebellion against the British.

1783 At the end of the Revolutionary War, Michigan becomes a part of the United States.

1787 Michigan becomes part of the Northwest Territory.

1796 General Anthony Wayne and his troops take over Detroit after the Jay Treaty is signed.

1805 The Michigan Territory is created. Detroit is almost completely destroyed by fire.

1807 The Treaty of Detroit is signed, taking a large section of southeastern Michigan away from Native Americans and giving it to settlers.

1808 Father Gabriel Richard brings a printing press to Detroit and founds Michigan's school system.

1812 The British capture Detroit during the War of 1812.

1837 Michigan becomes the 26th state of the Union.

1844 Iron ore is discovered near Negaunee.

1854 Antislavery forces form a Republican party at Jackson.

1855 The Soo Canal is opened at Sault Sainte Marie.

1896 The first automobile rolls down the streets of Detroit.

1903 Henry Ford opens the Ford Motor Company in Detroit.

1920 Detroit's WWJ, the first commercial radio station in the nation, begins broadcasting regular programs.

1943 Riots caused by racial tensions break out in Detroit.

1957 The Mackinac Bridge is completed, linking the Upper and Lower peninsulas.

1967 Rioting breaks out in Detroit. Forty-three people die, and property damage runs in the millions of dollars.

1968 The state legislature passes an open-housing law that forbids racial, religious, or ethnic discrimination in housing.

1974 Vice President Gerald Ford of Michigan becomes the 38th President of the United States when President Richard Nixon resigns.

1977 The Renaissance Center, a renewal project in downtown Detroit, opens for business.

1990 Coleman Young is elected to his fifth term as mayor of Detroit.

1994 The city of Detroit qualifies for Federal Empowerment Zone, which awards tax breaks and grants.

In the center of the flag is the state seal. At the top of the seal is a banner with the words *E Pluribus Unum,* which means "From Many, One." A bald eagle representing the United States is perched on a shield bearing the word *Tuebor,* which means "I will defend." Below, an explorer looks at the horizon. A moose and an elk, which represent Michigan, are supported by a banner showing the state motto.

Michigan Almanac

Nickname. The Wolverine State

Capital. Lansing

State Bird. Robin

State Flower. Apple blossom

State Tree. White pine

State Motto. *Si quaeris peninsulam amoenam circumspice* (If you seek a pleasant peninsula, look about you.)

State Song. "Michigan, My Michigan"

State Abbreviations. Mich. (traditional); MI (postal)

Statehood. January 26, 1837, the 26th state

Government. Congress: U.S. senators, 2; U.S. representatives, 16. State Legislature: senators, 38; representatives; 110. Counties: 83

Area. 58,513 sq mi (151,548 sq km), 23rd in size among the states

Greatest Distances. north/south, 455 mi (732 km); east/west, 400 mi (640 km)

Elevation. Highest: Mount Curwood, 1,980 ft (604 m). Lowest: 572 ft (174 m), along Lake Erie

Population. 1990 Census: 9,328,784 (1% increase over 1970), 8th among the states. Density: 159 persons per sq mi (62 persons per sq km). Distribution: 70% urban, 30% rural. 1980 Census: 9,258,344

Economy. *Agriculture:* corn, winter wheat, soybeans, dry beans, blueberries, beef cattle, hogs, milk. *Fishing:* chub, whitefish. *Manufacturing:* transportation equipment, automobiles, machinery, fabricated metal products, food products, chemicals. *Mining:* iron ore, petroleum, natural gas

State Bird: Robin

State Flower: Apple blossom

Annual Events

* ★ Snow Fly in Kalamazoo (January)
* ★ Maple Syrup Festival in Bloomfield Hills (March)
* ★ National Morel Mushroom Hunting Championship in Boyne City (May)
* ★ World's Longest Breakfast Table in Battle Creek (June)
* ★ Lasers on the Lake in Muskegon (July)
* ★ Jazz and Harvest Festival in Buchanan (September)
* ★ Red Flannel Festival in Cedar Springs (October)

Places to Visit

* ★ Fort Michilimackinac in Mackinaw City
* ★ Greenfield Village in Dearborn
* ★ Museum of African American History in Detroit
* ★ Pictured Rocks National Lakeshore, near Munsing
* ★ Sleeping Bear Dune National Lakeshore, near Frankfort
* ★ Soo Canal, at Sault Sainte Marie
* ★ Tahquamenon Falls, near Newberry
* ★ Windmill Island Municipal Park in Holland

State Seal

Index

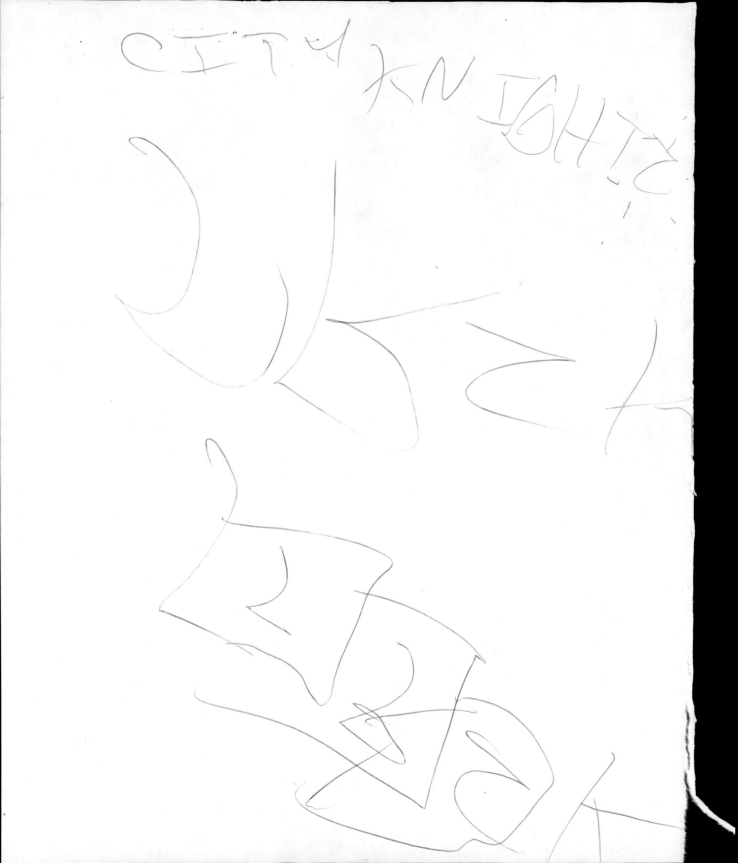